A LITTLE KEYBOARD BOOK

A Little Keyboard Book

EIGHT TUNES OF COLONIAL VIRGINIA

Set for Piano or Harpsichord

by

J. S. DARLING

*Organist and Choirmaster of Bruton Parish Church
in Williamsburg, Harpsichordist and Musical
Consultant to Colonial Williamsburg*

The Colonial Williamsburg Foundation

Williamsburg, Virginia

Thirteenth Printing, 2001

ISBN 0–910412–93–6
Library of Congress Catalog Card No. 71–165364

Printed in the United States of America

PREFACE

THESE EIGHT PIECES are taken from the manuscript music books of the Bollings, once of Chellowe plantation, Buckingham County, Virginia. They now form part of the Hubard Family Papers, in the Southern Historical Collection, University of North Carolina Library, whose kind permission to publish these selections is gratefully acknowledged.

The Bolling music may be called a typical assemblage of the popular music of the decades before and after the American Revolution. The inclusion of pieces by mid-eighteenth-century composers like Handel, Felton, and Tartini indicates that the collection may well have been begun by Robert Bolling (1738-1775). He was educated at Wakefield School in Yorkshire, England, studied law with Benjamin Waller in the late 1750s, and represented his county in the House of Burgesses in Williamsburg. Other tunes were probably written out by Powhatan Bolling (1767-1802), son of Robert, who was an "ardent violinist," and by his brother Linnaeus (1773-1849), the composer of the *Cannonade at Yorktown*. Many of the pieces are anonymous and may well have been composed by one of the Bollings. Of particular interest is the Minuet by Peter Pelham, the only piece known at present to have been written by the first organist of Bruton Parish Church.

The music was intended for violin, but to reach a wider audience today I have arranged the pieces in eighteenth-century styles for keyboard instruments: harpsichord, piano, or chamber organ. The melodies have not been changed in any way, and it would be highly appropriate for a violin to play the melody along with the harpsichord. Except for the *Cannonade at Yorktown* and the *Minuet* the composers are not presently known, although Mr. George P. Carroll, formerly bandmaster of Colonial Williamsburg, has identified the *Trumpet March* as an anonymous German military tune of about 1760.

Special thanks are due to Dr. John W. Molnar of Longwood College, Farmville, Virginia, who called the attention of Colonial Williamsburg to these music manuscripts and conducted research into the Bolling family history.

Music was a popular diversion of our colonial forebears, and these sprightly pieces retain their freshness and charm two centuries later.

J. S. DARLING
Organist, Bruton Parish Church
Musical Consultant, Colonial Williamsburg

CONTENTS

A Preface by Mr. Darling v

Trumpet March 1

Minuet by Mr. Pelham 3

Patterson's Hornpipe 6

Cannonade at Yorktown 8

Pease upon a Trencher 10

Congo — A Jig 11

Windsor Forest — A Hornpipe 12

Lord Loudoun's March 14

TRUMPET MARCH

tr.

MINUET BY MR. PELHAM

Organist of the Church in Williamsburg

Forte
Forte
4

Forte
Piano
Forte

PATTERSON'S HORNPIPE

CANNONADE AT YORKTOWN

L. Bolling — 1792

PEASE UPON A TRENCHER

CONGO—A JIG

WINDSOR FOREST—A HORNPIPE

LORD LOUDOUN'S MARCH

tr.
tr.
tr.

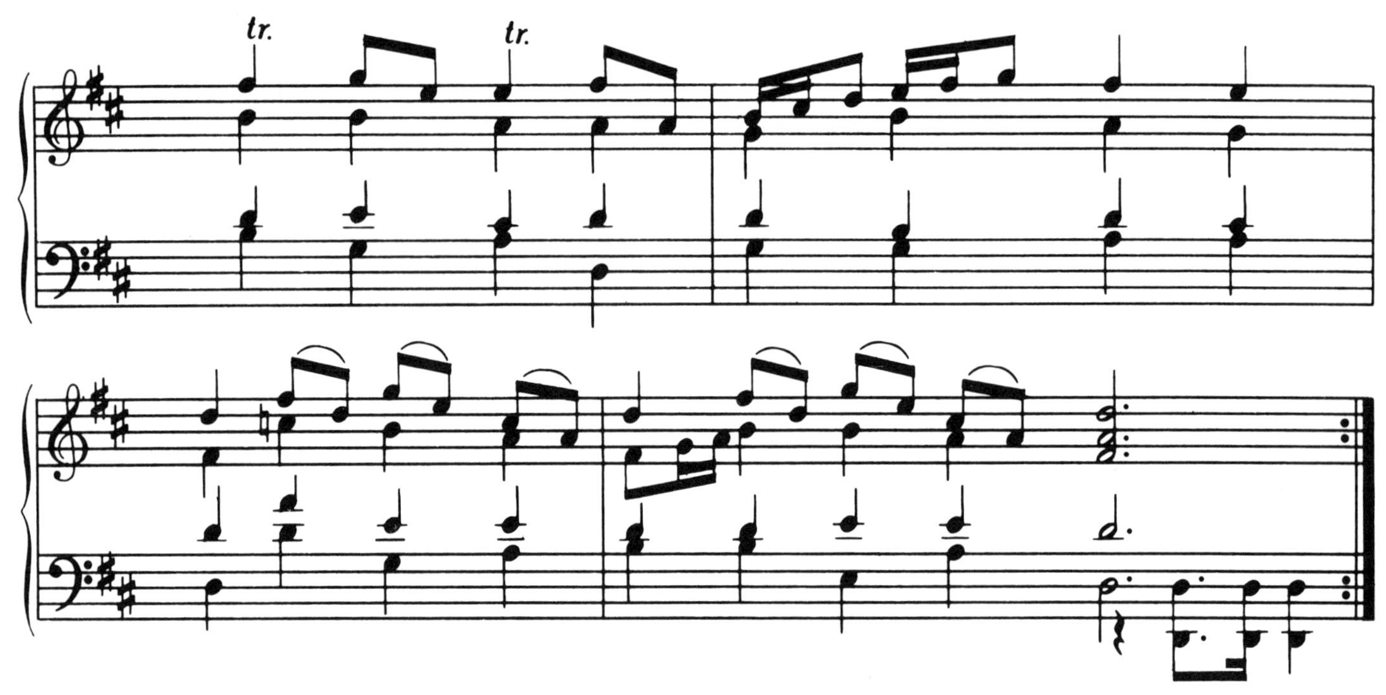